100 PARENTING TIPS INSPIRED BY ADOLESCENCE

DR DHEERAJ MEHROTRA

Contents

Foreword

Presented herein are 100 parenting strategies derived from insights gained from Netflix's mini-series Adolescence, emphasising themes such as male aggression, incel culture, socioeconomic challenges, and the influence of the digital era on a working-class family exemplified by Jamie Miller. The series, conceived by Jack Thorne and Stephen Graham, underscores the tribulations of a 13-year-old child charged with the murder of his classmate, along with the ensuing repercussions on his family and community. These recommendations are pragmatic, contemplative, and designed to assist parents in managing the intricacies of child-rearing in contemporary society, focusing on emotional support, communication, and awareness of socio-economic and digital influences.

Preface

Parenting is not a science—it's an evolving journey of love, patience, learning, and growing alongside your child. 100 Parenting Tips Inspired by Adolescence is based on the many real-life lessons, reflections, and experiences of navigating the dynamic and often challenging teenage years.

Adolescence is a transformative phase, not only for children but for parents, too. Children begin to shape their identities, question norms, and explore independence during this time. As parents, the role shifts from being mere caretakers to becoming guides, mentors, and silent pillars of strength. This book aims to support that transition.

The tips curated in this book are strategies and gentle reminders of empathy, connection, consistency, and understanding. Each tip is inspired by the beautiful complexity of teenage behavior and parents' deep desire to raise emotionally intelligent, resilient, and responsible young adults.

Whether you're a first-time parent of a teen

or someone revisiting the phase with another child, this book offers practical advice, reassurance, and a reminder that you are not alone in this journey.

Let this book be your companion in parenting, not just with discipline but with heart.

— Dr. Dheeraj Mehrotra

Prologue

Netflix's Adolescence, a gripping four-episode mini-series released on March 13, 2025, has captivated audiences with many views

globally. Created by Jack Thorne and Stephen Graham, who also stars as Eddie Miller, the show begins with a jarring scene: police storming into the home of 13-year-old Jamie Miller (Owen Cooper) to arrest him for murdering his classmate, Katie. Filmed in continuous single takes, the series unfolds in real time, immersing viewers in the chaos and emotional wreckage of a working-class family thrust into crisis. The story explores more than just a crime—it delves into male rage, incel culture, and the pressures of social media on today's youth. Jamie's parents, Eddie and Manda (Christine Tremarco), grapple with shock and guilt, questioning their role as their son's life unravels. A pivotal moment in Episode 1 captures their raw vulnerability: Eddie snaps at Manda for texting, only to learn she's securing their now-doorless home. The series peaks in Episode 3 with Jamie's chilling session with a psychologist (Erin Doherty), revealing how online misogyny and rejection fueled his actions, culminating in his guilty plea in Episode 4 on Eddie's birthday—a day marred by grief. For parents, Adolescence is a stark wake-up call. It highlights the hidden dangers of the digital world—where coded emojis and toxic forums can radicalize a child under your roof. It's a strict watch (rated TV-MA), but it is vital for understanding the crisis of modern boyhood. Key takeaways? Monitor online activity, foster open talks, and model empathy at home. While not every teen is Jamie, the series urges vigilance and connection to bridge the gap between generations and prevent tragedy. It's less a whodunit, more a "why",—and a must-see for parents navigating today's complex landscape.

ONE

100 Tips

———❦———

Building Emotional Awareness and Support

1. Check in with your child daily and enquire about their feelings, even on average.

2. Validate Emotions and assure them that it is acceptable to be angry or sad; do not disregard their feelings.

3. Instruct Emotional Naming: Help them name their feelings (for example, "frustrated" as opposed to "mad").

4. Demonstrate Calmness: Demonstrate how you can handle tension without losing your cool, much like Eddie does at the beginning.

5. Recognise Warning Signs: Pay attention to those who retreat, such as Jamie when he is in his room.

6. Encourage Expression: Present secure channels (art, conversation) for expressing emotions.

7. To avoid shaming anger, direct it into words rather than punish it.

8. To be present, you must spend time with them rather than be around them.

9. Listen First: Listening to what others say before making any decisions or offering any answers is essential.

10. Teach them coping skills by showing them techniques such as counting or breathing when experiencing difficulties.

Examining the Issues of Male Rage and Identity

11. Reframe the concept of strength by teaching young men that it encompasses more than simply toughness.

12. Confrontation of Stereotypes: Discuss how genuine men respect all individuals.

13. Discuss the concept of masculinity by enquiring about what they see as the characteristics of a "man" and then unpacking those characteristics.

14. Encourage Vulnerability: You should compliment them for sharing their concerns or uncertainties.

15. Steer clear of the phrase "toughen up": Do not force them to conceal their feelings because it will only grow.

16. Be a role model for respect by treating others, particularly women, with kindness.

17. Dig deeper than surface fights and investigate the origins of anger by asking why someone is angry.

18. Offer Outlets: Activities such as sports or hobbies can be a constructive energy channel.

19. Have a Conversation About Power: Explain that having power does not mean invading other people.

20. It is important to highlight positive men and share stories about sympathetic male figures.

Navigating the Online World and Incel Culture

21. Be Familiar with Their Applications: Familiarize yourself with the platforms that they use; do not remain like Eddie and Manda.

22. Set Screen Limits: Resolve to refrain from using mobile devices in bedrooms after a predetermined time.

23. Ask them who they follow and why they do so. Discuss the influence of the internet.

24. Teach Critical Thinking: This involves assisting students in questioning harmful concepts such as the "manosphere."

25. Describe the risks. Discuss how hatred expressed online can turn feelings of isolation into anger.

26. Monitor covertly: Check in without snooping; establish confidence first.

27. Teach others by example by limiting the amount of time you spend on your phone.

28. Be on the lookout for unexpected alterations in language or attitude to identify acts of radicalisation.

29. Foster Genuine Connections for People: Make an effort to make friends in person rather than in online echo chambers.

30. Discuss Gender Lies: Use data to dispel myths about gender, such as the notion that "women only like jerks."

Addressing the Problems of Socioeconomic Stress and Class

31. Recognise Struggles: Be truthful about the challenges you face at work or with money, and do it in an age-appropriate manner.

32. Teach them that effort is more important than wealth or prestige, creating pride.

33. Avoid Blame: Avoid allowing children to feel responsible for the family's stress, such as Jamie's parents' distraction.

34. Provide Stability: Maintain consistent habits, even amid turmoil (no front door).

35. Present Opportunities: Show them ways to go beyond the environment that is immediately surrounding them.

36. Discuss Class: Describe how society isn't always fair but how people can succeed despite this.

37. Encourage Dreams: Despite having socioeconomic limitations, assist them in aiming high.

38. Ease the pressure of shame by assuring them that their value is not dependent on money or "stuff."

39. Share experiences of overcoming difficult circumstances and encourage others to do the same.

40. Join the Community: Connect them to local groups to give them a feeling of belonging.

Strengthening Communication Within the Family

41. Put your phone down and discuss the topic without interruptions, in contrast to Manda's minute of texting.

42. Remain Calm in a Crisis: Instead of losing your cool like Eddie, take a deep breath.

43. Instead of asking, "Are you okay?" ask open-ended questions like, "What happened today?"

44. It is acceptable to admit that you are clueless, as Eddie does, and to say things like "I don't know yet."

45. Avoid ridiculing the public by keeping family matters private and not broadcasting them.

46. Resolve Fights: Instead of being silent, work through disagreements by apologising to one another.

47. Express Your Emotions: It's normal to feel emotional; crying or worrying is okay.

48. Become a team and tackle challenges together, just like the Millers did while they were at the station.

49. Chats should be scheduled in advance so that you can catch up regularly.

50. Hear Their Side: Even when disagreeing, hear what they say.

Developing Social Skills and Empathy in Children

51. Reward acts of kindness towards other people to teach kindness.

52. Role-Play Empathy: Acquire the skills necessary to respond to the suffering of a friend.

53. Discuss bullying: Enquire whether or not they have witnessed it at school and how they feel about it.

54. Encourage Inclusion: Influence them to invite the "outsider" to join in.

55. Talk about Katie and use her narrative to investigate the impact that being a victim has.

56. Practice Apologies: Demonstrate how to apologise honestly.

57. Applaud Cooperation: They should be praised for working well with others.

58. It is essential to investigate the reasons behind someone's behaviour and to dissect it.

59. Help them appreciate the word "no" from their peers by teaching them boundaries.

60. Establish friendships by setting up playdates or other events for the group.

Reacting to Emergencies and Traumatic Events

61. Face surprises as a family, such as Jamie's arrest, and remain united in the face of them.

62. Explain Systems: Break down the legal or police stuff straightforwardly.

63. Allow Grief: Letting someone cry or become angry is not a sign of weakness.

64. Seek Assistance: Seek counselling if the behaviour does not improve.

65. Be truthful: Share what you know rather than spreading rumours.

66. Assure their safety by assuring them that you will protect them even amid chaos.

67. Process Together: Discuss significant events after the dust has settled.

68. In the event of a crisis, you should avoid pointing the finger of blame at them.

**69. Remain Physically Close: Hugs are something that should be given.
Show them there is a way to move forward by planning the next steps.**

70. Keeping people from becoming radicalised and isolated

71. Fill Their Time: Activities are preferable to browsing endlessly on any device.

72. Get to Know Their Crew: Speak with family and friends.

73. Identify Loneliness: Inquire as to whether or not they experience feelings of being excluded in any way.

74. Develop a sense of self-worth by frequently praising their strengths.

75. Educate people that harbouring hatred is not a solution to any problem.

76. Participate in Hobbies: Determine what excites them and go right in.

77. Reduce time spent alone and maintain a healthy balance between time spent alone and with family.

78. Discuss Belonging: Inquire about where they believe they belong.

79. Keep an eye out for secrets: If they are concealing their internet life, gently explore them.

80. Provide Mentors: They should be connected to grownups who are trusted beyond you.

Fostering Accountability and Growth in Individuals

81. Their Errors: Instruct them to acknowledge when they are in the wrong.

82. Establish Consequences: You should link acts to equitable results.

83. You should discuss Jamie's choice and ask them what they would do differently.

84. Teach Repair: Demonstrate how to repair the damage they cause.

85. Applaud Effort: Pay attention to striving rather than only winning.

86. Set Goals: Assist them in planning for modest victories.

87. Discuss Responsibility: Describe how decisions affect one's life.

88. The question "What did you learn today?" is a great way to encourage reflection.

89. Model Growth: Discuss how you have grown as an individual.

90. Build grit by encouraging children to persevere in adversity.

Bridging the Gap in the Classroom Discussion

91. Challenge Labels: Dispel falsehoods that are "demonising" regarding their history from their perspective.

92. Show them that there are worlds outside their street by exposing them to diversity.

93. Discussing the media, ask what the adolescent era has to say about social class.

94. Value the effort that you put in: Success should be tied to effort, not privilege.

95. If you want to address inequality, you should explain why some people have more than others.

96. Teach advocacy by demonstrating many ways to advocate for fairness.

97. Stay away from envy by concentrating on their journey rather than the things of others.

98. Discuss the heroes of the working class.

99. Instill Hope: Reassure them that their social status does not limit their future.

100. Unite as Equals: Show every child the same respect.

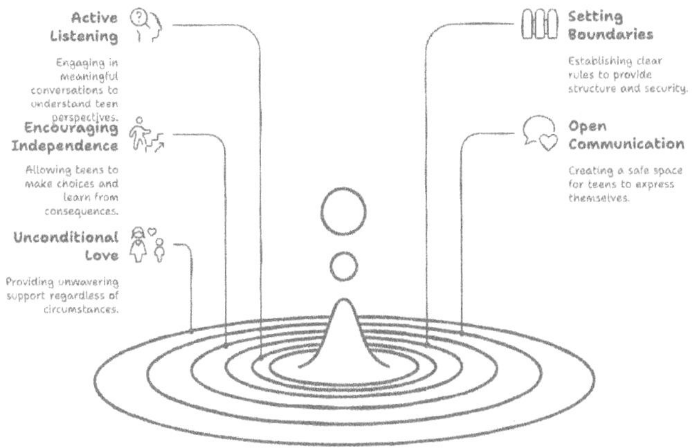

Guiding Adolescents with Love

Communication
Encouraging open dialogue and active listening to build trust.

Boundaries
Establishing clear limits to provide structure and safety.

Independence
Fostering self-reliance and decision-making skills in teens.

Support
Providing emotional and practical support during adolescence.

Growth
Encouraging personal development and resilience.

Scan Here
FOR QUALITY BOOKS
For Home Library for
Parents, Educators &Students

About The Author

Dr. Dheeraj Mehrotra is a distinguished educational leader and innovator with over three decades of experience transforming education through excellence and innovation. A recipient of the President of India's National Teacher Award (2006), he is a certified expert in Six Sigma (White and Yellow Belt), Neuro-Linguistic Programming (NLP), and Total Quality Management (TQM). His specialisation encompasses academic audits, school quality assurance and accreditation (SQAA), and implementing Kaizen and 5S in schools. As an accomplished author, Dr. Mehrotra has published over 200 books on various subjects, including computer science, artificial intelligence, digital body language, quality circles, and school management. His contributions also include the development of more than 150 free educational mobile apps for teachers, students, and parents, a feat recognised by the Limca Book of Records and the India Book of Records. Dr. Mehrotra has served as Principal at prestigious institutions such as De Indian Public School in New Delhi, NPS International School in Guwahati, and Kunwar's Global School in Lucknow. He has also held the position of Education Officer at GEMS in Gurgaon, making significant contributions to the global education community. As a premier UDEMY instructor, Dr. Mehrotra has created over 500 courses that have impacted more than 800,000 learners across 180 countries. Additionally, as the founder and president of the IoT Society of India, he advocates for technology integration in education worldwide.